IT'S NOT ABOUT ME

7 Key Principles for the Heart of Corporate America

RANDALL HAUG

Hiromi,

Spread the word!

—RH

STREAMLINE
BOOKS

Contents

Preface   vii
Introduction   ix

1. Servant Leadership   1
   With Jeff Ward
2. Perception   13
   With Gilberto Garcia
3. Perspective   23
   with Doug Voss
4. Sacrifice   33
   With Jim Hildreth
5. Leading Questions   43
   With Brent Witthuhn
6. Mistakes   55
   With Three Giants of Leadership
7. Wisdom   69
   With King Solomon

Afterword   81
Acknowledgments   83
Notes   85

For my parents, Greg and Lina—who gave selflessly to make sure I am the leader I strive to be today.

Thank you.

Preface

"There is one quality which one must possess to win, and that is definiteness of purpose, the knowledge of what one wants and a burning desire to achieve it."
—Napoleon Hill

My leadership journey from baseball, to a Catholic high school for boys, to Shred-it, to UCA College of Business, to a Fortune 500 company has been a dynamic one. There are countless stories that embody that journey and my dream for explaining how to truly live like **It's Not About Me**. For our purposes I am going to explain the most impactful ones that lead to the inception of this book.

The first Haug to enter this country was my grandpa, August Haug. He came from Wurmlinger-Rottersburg, Germany in 1871, and eventually settled in St. Benedict, Kansas. He married and had 15 kids (what a life that

must have been). I didn't have the chance to know
August, but with fathering 15 kids he likely lived a life
that wasn't about him, and he definitely didn't have time
to live a life that was about him.

The oldest living Haug, that everyone is aware of, is
Ralph Haug. There are a ton of stories about my
Grandpa and our time together. I cherish those moments
that I had with him as they taught me so much.

He is the epitome of a true leader. He won't tell you
that, but I grew up recognizing the leader that he is, was,
and will continue to be. He met my grandmother, Mary
Alice, when he was 18 and they were married at 19. He
gave her the world. I will be forever grateful to both of
them.

Thank you.

Introduction

"What really *is* leadership? And why am I writing a book about it?"

Those questions (or some form of them) aren't just ones I ask myself regularly—they're questions that others have asked me in recent months.

Through ~30 short years on earth, my life has been touched by some wildly influential individuals. That is an interesting way to think about things, right? To some degree, that is true about everyone, but not everyone thinks that way.

And maybe more than the individuals themselves, it's the *words* they have spoken into my life that have made all the difference. Words are so powerful.

What I want to accomplish in this introduction is to set the stage for the influential people in my life that helped create the person I am today, and the leadership lessons that corporate America would do good to take to heart. The importance of these individuals starts with a reality conveyed to me years ago:

People are the average of the 7 people they surround themselves with on a consistent basis.

You may have heard some form or fashion of that statement. Some say five and others say ten, but regardless . . . there is so much meaning behind the phrase itself. We will dive into that more later.

Yet there was *another* individual, when discussing the phrase, who took it a step further. He said "Yes, you are the average of the 7 people you surround yourself with the most, **but also the 7 people you think about negatively the most."**

That original phrase obviously struck a chord with me, but that add-on, about how much we think about others in a negative light, is the sad truth not many of us want to confront.

In summary, **people are the average of the 7 positive (+) and 7 negative (-) people that have made a lasting impression on them throughout their lives.**

I believe that is true for every person that walks on Earth, but most might not think of it this way. Every leader should be aware of, and keep track of those 14 individuals. Why? Because as new people enter your life, and other people *leave* your life, that list can change. (Sometimes multiple times in the same week, month, or year). As you think about your list right this second—if you don't like someone who is on it, that's OK. They don't have to stay there forever.

The people we surround ourselves with (or allow to take up mental headspace) affect our emotional and literal well-being..

I am so grateful that you have decided to read this book. My hope is that you will not only learn impactful leadership principles through the stories I share, but that you will feel moved to apply them to all aspects of your life.

Thank you for taking the time to read it.

Books are great. But there's nothing better than real life interaction, and I hope to meet you face-to-face some-day. I'd love to grab coffee and hear about your thoughts on the book. In the meantime, if you have any questions or comments while reading *It's Not About Me*, please contact me at www.RandallHaug.com.

Every word that follows is the result of my 14. The good, the bad, and those who cared enough about me to tell me like it is. When you have those kinds of people in your corner, you're that much closer to a life that isn't about you.

Servant Leadership
WITH JEFF WARD

"Success is not final, failure is not fatal: it is the courage to continue that counts."
—Winston Churchill

There's something profoundly impactful about those first few "coaches" we have in our earliest years of organized sports or activities. Even if it just looks like a herd of cats chasing a ball around a field, that first coach or two is often the first person (outside of your parents or care-givers) who has an opportunity to encourage us and help us get better at something.

I have known Jeff Ward since I was eight-years-old— he was one of my first coaches in little league baseball. His oldest son, Tanner, and I grew up playing baseball together and went to high school together. We even went to the same college, and spent a year as roommates. Therefore, Jeff and I have stayed in touch over the last 20 years which is crazy to even think about. He has held many different titles in my life: coach, mentor, boss, and most importantly a friend. Allow me a quick word for Jeff alone:

Thank you, Mr. Ward, for making such a positive impact on the leader I've become. I truly wouldn't be here without your help, guidance, and encouragement..

In 2011, when I was a senior in high school, I worked at a confidential-document destruction company, Shred-it. It was a franchised operation, and you might have guessed—Jeff Ward owned the location in my hometown of Maumelle, Arkansas. We shredded confidential documents for companies, sold the shredded paper to *other* companies, who then recycled it back into paper. Yes, to some degree, I was a professional "paper pusher." As a teenager, I enjoyed my time at Shred-it because it paid well—the job itself took place in a warehouse and *did* require some physical labor, but we didn't have to work late into the nights like most teenagers did at restaurants in town. I was given numerous opportunities to make extra money by working on the weekends shredding massive amounts of documents for customers that didn't have a regular service.

While working overtime during one of those weekends, Jeff taught me a defining lesson I have carried with me throughout a young career in corporate America.

Although I indeed signed up to work on a Saturday, my attitude was less than voluntary on the actual day of work. I remember pulling into the parking with an attitude, but just thought I'd grind out the day to make some extra cash. I couldn't believe it when I got out of my car and looked up to Jeff's car in the parking lot. We were two of the only cars there.

"What is the owner doing here on a Saturday?" I thought to myself.

I walked inside of the warehouse and saw Jeff moving some boxes. I first asked him if everything was OK, and then looked around the warehouse to notice the first bulk of work—work I was supposed to get done that Saturday—was already complete. Then I noticed something else: Jeff was sweating profusely.

"Who did all this?" I asked, but could probably have guessed.

He replied with a light chuckle: "I did."

I stood there looking at my best friend's dad—the man I first knew as "coach" and now knew as "boss." And quite frankly, I couldn't believe it. How could someone of that caliber lower himself to this kind of work on a Saturday? Didn't he have something more important on his calendar? or a vacation calling his name? The next words that came from Jeff's mouth are words that altered the course of my career aspirations and attitude.

"Randall," said Jeff, "a good leader will never tell his team to do anything he hasn't done before and is above doing himself. Remember that."

That powerful lesson was my first lesson on servant leadership. Every opportunity I get to lead a group of individuals, I ask myself, "Have I done what I'm asking them to do?"

A good leader *has* performed that team's job and knows enough about it that he or she could lead and motivate them on how to improve it. Of course, that's just the short version of how servant leadership can positively impact any workplace. For a little more description, I invited Jeff himself to expound on the principles of servant leadership.

Jeff sent me three parts that speak to a more important whole. The first part is persuasion, and how we can gently steer others in an effort to bring out their best selves and work for the good of the team.

Persuade with Caution (Jeff Ward)

Servant Leadership is an interesting style of leading an organization. Unfortunately, in today's day-in-age — and the way this term has become so well known— many corporate leaders and executives like to think of themselves as servant leaders.

The problem, as many of us know, is that some of them truly are servant leaders, while others clearly are not. The best servant leaders I know in the corporate space encourage curiosity and creativity. Anyone would want those qualities in an employee, but it takes time to draw them out of someone. It's like when a parent spends time explaining something to their child, only for the child to respond with "Why?" after every word of instruction given. Children are (typically) engaged and want to understand, but other times you just want them to put their damn seatbelt on! So, servant leadership training says a leader must improve one's persuasion skills. Persuasion means being able to convince others that your thinking is the right path—or at least a path in the right and general direction. But this is where the word "servant" comes in because unlike other forms of leadership (and there are some bad ones), persuasion through the lens of servant leadership often uses no words at all. And boy, can it take some time to catch on.

It Takes Time

The first time I heard Jeff talk about servant leadership as persuasion, I had to reframe my way of thinking. Servant leadership *is* a buzzword in business. However, in the corporate space leaders oftentimes do worse than just buzzing about it. They talk the talk, but have a hard time walking it out in real life. I, for one, am guilty of this. Sometimes we just want to scream at our employees to, in Jeff's words, "put the damn seatbelt on!" (Or whatever the daily task's equivalent is). But servant leadership takes time to cultivate. It may take months or even years tilling the land, so that our businesses might reap the harvest later on.

Jeff transitions to his second key point of wisdom that

involves a story about his relationship with his father. Whether it's a mom, dad, or grandparent, those first primary caregivers are often our first examples of servant leadership or, unfortunately, lack thereof.

Words from Dad Stick (Jeff Ward)

For most of my upbringing, my dad was *anything but* a servant leader. It was his way or the highway. I'd be lying if I said some of that didn't rub off on me while parenting my own children as they grew up. It's crazy how you catch yourself slowly over time becoming the things you didn't enjoy growing up. My father passed away in 2006, and it was just two days after I signed an agreement to buy my first company. I always felt it was my dad's way of saying, "Okay Jeff, you're good to go. Now go kick some ass!"

So, although my father was a bit hard-headed, and I wouldn't classify him as a "servant leader" of sorts, he did implement a kind of servant leadership style. He'd ask questions, and later come back for my answer in order to educate me on a topic. That question and answer format turned into a healthy conversation more often than not.

For example, when I turned 17-years-old, I informed him I wanted to move in with a friend who was a year older than me. My friend had graduated high school and I was a senior. You would think his answer would have been "Hell no" or "Don't let the door hit you on the way out." Instead, he said "Let me think about it and we can discuss the possibilities later."

As I look back on that moment as an adult, it's the day I started viewing my dad as the servant leader that was somewhere inside of him. It's a moment that led me to believe there is a servant leader in *all* of us—again, it just takes time and persistence to cultivate. He asked my mom to get some specific items when she was getting groceries that day. He later called me into his home office and sat me down. He was sitting at his rolltop desk that I now have in my home office. He slid a receipt over to me with a number of items with a checkmark next to them. Toothpaste, check. Old Spice Deodorant, check. Toilet paper, check. Paper towels, check. And on he went.

"OK, what's this all about, Dad?" I said.

He told me how those were just a few of the items that my mother and him would pay for each time I needed them. He then asked if I had thought about how I would pay for other items when I moved in with my friend. Needless to say, I hunkered down at my parents a little while longer. Not only did he use persuasion as a form of servant leadership, but he displayed great patience with me in the process—not getting mad for proposing a new thought or idea.

People Can Change

The stories we hold onto with our parents are crazy, aren't they? I think it's an amazing thing when someone opens up about the moments they hold onto from their youth. Jeff is a grown adult and successful businessman, but it was that moment with his dad that started Jeff down *his own* path of servant leadership.

Another thing that sticks out is that Jeff admittedly says his dad wasn't a servant leader for most of his life. But a beautiful part of the story is that his dad learned to change. People change. People *can* change, as long as you can find what motivates them to do so and the benefit behind it.

Ask Questions. Empathize. Repeat. (Jeff Ward)

Nothing in life will impact one's leadership style—in the corporate space or business in general—more than being 1) a parent or 2) a coach. If you have been either of those things, you know those experiences directly correlate to being a leader. While many have had a parent and/or a coach in their lives, there are just as many who unfortunately didn't have a stable role model in their life. Some of those people also didn't participate in organized sports or activities. For that reason—everyone comes from a different background

—I have incorporated a unique set of interview questions I ask prospective employees.

One of those questions is "What is a time you've disagreed with your parents or guardian, and how did you handle the situation? A lot of them look at me at first as if they walked into a counseling session instead of a job interview. I've learned over the years that for as easy as it is to get frustrated with some of their responses, it's important to realize their parents (in most cases) were just doing the best they knew how to do.

Some employees make it through that interview process, and some do not. For the ones who do, you're now in charge of stewarding them in one of two ways. The first, "my way or the highway" approach, or through servant leadership—empowering them to be curious and creative. Not *as* a good parent. That's not your job. But *like* a good parent. You have to engage, weekly if not daily, and ask questions to see what type of upbringing they had so that you understand the foundation each employee is operating from. If more leaders in the corporate space would operate this way, I'm positive we would see change, for the better, in the decades to come.

A Phrase Worth Repeating

In the same way I'm grateful Jeff served as my little league coach from the time I was eight, I'm just as thankful for these three points of wisdom underlying servant leadership.

Hearing him tell these lessons in person is even more impactful, but reading those words is a powerful experience in its own right. I couldn't think of a better way to kick off this book than Jeff sharing from his own point of view, and how his leadership deeply affected someone like me—who then gets to live out those principles alongside hundreds of individuals a week. I have learned something from him at every stage of my life, which leads me to a word that goes hand-in-hand with servant leadership: consistency.

Jeff has always been there for me when I needed him —contributing to this book included. When he helps me in work and life, he does so without asking for anything in return. It's that kind of mentality that embodies a phrase our society needs to play on repeat: "**It's Not About Me**."

Say it again. Over and over. *"It's not about me."* And when you put this book down today, recall those four words throughout your day.

"It's not about me."

And when you repeat those words to yourself, how will their truth affect your actions? How might the people around you, at any given moment, benefit from you repeating those words to yourself?

Jeff agreed to contribute to this book because we both believe it's an opportunity to get that message out into the corporate world. Who would've thought that a random Saturday of working overtime would lead to such a life-altering event? As a ticked-off teenager, it's certainly not what I expected. But when individuals like Jeff Ward pave the way, in business and life, through servant leadership, sometimes the unexpected turns into the extraordinary.

2

Perception
WITH GILBERTO GARCIA

"The secret to getting ahead is getting started."
—Mark Twain

In my final semester of college, I had to take a "Business Policy and Strategy" class that met once a week, on Mondays, from 6-9 pm. Not only was it a tough class, but taking it once a week for three hours all at once, after your brain was already fried from school all day, made it even more mind numbing.

That class is where I met Gilberto.

I remember walking in and sitting at a table in the front of the class by myself with another guy sitting by himself at the table behind me. He was definitely an athlete because he was a big dude. He and I became friends pretty early on into the class and actually ended up doing a class project together. The reason Gilberto and I became such good friends is because we both have a similar drive in business, but more importantly share the burning desire to make a positive impact in other peoples' lives. Gilberto is a wealth management advisor for Northwestern Mutual and tracks his success not by *dollars sold* but by *lives impacted*. He truly believes it's not about him and that's the positive force that drives all his success. (He is my financial advisor as well).

Gilberto, thank you for the friendship over the years and the conversations about the future. I look forward to more of those to come.

Google defines perception as "a way of regarding, understanding, or interpreting something; a mental impression." I love that because we as humans perceive hundreds of things each day in a positive or negative way. Gilberto has a fun anecdote that altered his perception forever, and oddly enough . . . also altered the way he views ants.

No Doubts Whatsoever (Gilberto Garcia)

To start, this concept was introduced to me playing Division One FCS football at the University of Central Arkansas (UCA) in 2016 by head coach Steve Campbell. Coach Campbell went on to lead UCA to the first ever back to back 10 win seasons in school history, and resulted in UCA being the number 3 team in the entire country. During Coach Campbell's 30 year tenure, he never had a losing season, and won two national championships.

In the fall of 2016 while playing as an offensive lineman, I experienced one of the most surreal moments during (what was supposed to be) a typical film session. Coach Campbell was leading the session when he unexpectedly paused the film in the middle of a play, and turned toward our group. He stood in silence for a moment before asking us this question:

"If I gave you $1,000,000 to kill an ant, how would you do it?"

A few guys in the room chuckled, but others just stared right back at him—trying to process any kind of logical reply. Most of the initial answers were pretty simple: "I'd step on it" or "I'd press down my finger on it." Coach Campbell leaned back in his chair—very relaxed with his hands and arms on top of his head as he listened to more responses. Surprisingly, nobody focused on the $1,000,000 part. For most of the guys it was about killing the ant in the quickest, easiest way possible. He waited until the last response came then sat up quickly . . .

"NO!" he screamed— acting as if he was about to flip the table to grab everyone's attention.

"If someone was going to pay me $1,000,000 to kill an ant," Coach Campbell explained, "I would go to the bank, get a $200,000 loan to purchase a nuclear bomb, and then I would clear the entire area. I'd put my finger on it, step on it, and then blow it up so that by the end of day, there is *no doubt whatsoever* that the ant was completely dead. And I *still* net $800,000."

We all laughed as Coach Campbell often came up with hilarious analogies and metaphors—we now had another to add to the list.

"What I'm trying to say is that to blow up the ant is to not leave any doubt that you completed the task at hand."

He continued to explain how as offensive linemen we needed to make sure we blocked our assigned player on each play until the final whistle, so that we did everything we could possibly do to ensure success. I can't speak for my teammates, but I had no way of knowing, at that moment, how Coach Campbell's story on how to "Blow Up the Ant" would change my perception on business and life.

Ignite the Fire

From servant leadership to blowing up ants. I know Chapter 2 takes a distinct turn from Chapter 1. But I truly think the principles shared by Jeff Ward in Chapter 1 complement Gilberto's story, and experiences with Coach Campbell in an impactful way.

I've found that every great leader gets their motivation or "why" from impactful stories they came across or experienced. Whatever story they're telling may not have the same impact on everyone, but it had a lasting one on that leader. "Blow Up the Ant" ignited the fire in Gilberto's mind to help him become the best version of himself. What story or lesson created that drive for you?

Track Your Progress (Gilberto Garcia)

After I graduated from college and got started in the business world, lessons like "Blow Up the Ant" helped me transition to a high-intensity job—a 160-year-old, Fortune 100 company.

I've told the "Blow Up the Ant" story many times to friends, colleagues, and teams to help us all get on the same page. You might've heard "The person who *tracks* something the most will win", and I certainly believe that blowing up the ant is the best way to track goals and progress.

In corporate America, the goals our teams put into place are only as good as how we execute them. To accomplish those goals is taking the resources you've been given to ensure the best outcome—why settle for anything less than blowing up the ant? To blow up the ant in the corporate space is to possess a clear understanding of the goal itself and motivation around it. It means writing it down and looking at it often to make sure you don't forget it. *Actually* tracking the progress means checking on that goal daily. It means taking every measure to ensure there's no chance you miss your goal.

So if that's the "What" behind blowing up ants in business, what about the "How"?

Communication, in any team setting, is *crucial* to ensuring said team accomplishes their goal(s). Track the inventory, solidify every detail, and hold each other accountable every day, so that the end result is an ant blown into smithereens is inevitable. To blow up the ant is to get 1% better every single day. *That's* proper perception in the workplace. *That's* how you track progress in corporate America, and it pertains to qualitative goals (following up with new leads, respecting the opinions of others) as much as it does to quantitative goals (hitting sales goals, staying below budget). And when you *do* blow up the ant, and have a little bit of time, energy, and money leftover . . . take care of your people and teams. We've celebrated with week-long vacations (with employee families of course) and over-the-top dinners with good food and great people. It may not be the $800k Coach Campbell talked about, but it's more than enough to celebrate a job well done. And an ant that's 100% dead.

What Gets Tracked?

Gilberto teaches a very important lesson here. Tracking progress in the corporate space is an underrated skill for any professional, young or seasoned. Whether you are tracking your own or an employee's progress, you are doing so to improve results and make your team stronger. What gets tracked gets accomplished. Every business tracks sales year round to determine which campaigns or products increase sales. What works well is repeated. What doesn't work well is studied, so we can determine what went wrong and how it can be avoided in the future.

Seize the Opportunity While You Can (Gilberto Garcia)

Hopefully this "Blow Up the Ant" concept allows you to take the ceiling off of your goals, and remove any limits you have for yourself. Anytime you consider setting a new goal, or struggle to push an existing goal past the finish line, think about blowing up the ant using any resources at your disposal—it may not be $1,000,000 but it rarely needs to be. I'm willing to bet you have many resources and sources of support to complete whichever goal comes to mind. Set an "end goal" date and track your progress each calendar day until that date. Let others in on that goal, and even pay them if you have to. Do whatever it takes to make sure that ant doesn't somehow crawl away in the end.

Have a big interview in a couple days that could change your family's life? Set 10 alarms, do your research in the week prior on who is interviewing you, explain something that sets yourself apart from others, and leave no doubt that *you* are the right person for the job. Don't be intimidated by the magnitude of your goals, completely obliterate that ant. After all, we've all stepped on plenty of ants only to watch them come crawling out from under our shoes. In corporate America, too many of those ants crawling around might drive you up a wall, and send your job into jeopardy. Therefore, it's best you invest in the right kind of weaponry to take care of matters the first time.

Perception is a Choice

Such a funny and simple phrase: "Blow Up the Ant". But I hope Gilberto's lesson lodges itself somewhere in that brain of yours.

I have determined that there are two key ways to think about perception when it comes to accomplishing a goal or resolving a business solution:

1. Perception is a priority.
2. Perception is their reality.

The first way is pivotal because how you perceive any situation, task, goal, or endeavor determines how well or fast it gets done. Therefore, prioritize perception in any business setting or circumstance by taking a moment to pause before making a decision. "Pausing" could be for one minute, one hour, or even a whole day. Rarely do we *need* to make a split-second decision on anything, so take a moment to pause and perceive before making big *or* seemingly small decisions—it'll help you blow up the ant.

The second way I determined when entering corporate America and visiting customers for a living. What helped me quickly and effectively resolve my customers' issues was understanding that **It's Not About Me**. When I started putting my customers' needs first and putting myself in their shoes, I saw solutions that resulted in mutually beneficial, and longer lasting professional relationships.

If your customer feels you didn't give them a full understanding of what you're currently providing them with, or what you're trying to sell them, it's likely they'll be negatively affected by their experience with you. If you can change the way your customer perceives what you're selling, and how that will benefit them, you will see a dynamic change in how you resolve issues.

In other words, the best way to blow up the ant in business—by doing everything in your power to ensure a mutually beneficial interaction—is to remember: **It's Not About Me.**

3

Perspective
WITH DOUG VOSS

"We should remember that good fortune often happens when opportunity meets with preparation."

—Thomas Edison

The day I realized that fixing corporate America starts with fixing oneself is the day my life changed. It's also the day I met Dr. Doug Voss. Dr. Voss was my Transportation and Supply Chain Management professor at the University of Central Arkansas. He was the most personable of my college professors, and that was reflected in his teaching style. He did an exceptional job of getting to know us as people before he started to teach us as students. That seems to be an effective way to get people to buy into what you're selling, doesn't it? Connecting with people on a personal level is the best way to create long term relationships with them regardless of what industry you're in. That was Doug Voss. He was always very interested in what you wanted to do long term, whether it was in the supply chain field or not. He learned about you so that he could find the "hook", and that helped him teach you in a way that enabled learning and personal growth.

Aside from Doug being my college professor, he is also a good friend. He and I have kept in touch over the years. I speak to one of his classes every semester about my time as a fleet manager dealing with drivers and the Department of Transportation. I also spoke some about leadership, and how no matter what industry you're in or what company you work for, you have a responsibility to show up and give it 110% every single day.

Doug, thank you for the guidance over the years. I appreciate the leadership lessons you have taught me on a personal level and professional ones. I wouldn't have the confidence I have today without you. Thank you.

A Perspective Worth Repeating (Doug Voss)

"Don't eat your boogers. Don't eat your friends' boogers. Don't take any wooden nickels." These are the final sentences of a routine I go through with my kids each day when I drop them off at school. I started this routine because I kept repeating the same basic departures to them each morning and wanted to end it on a humorous note. Hence, boogers and nickels.

The first and most important part of our morning

routine goes like this: "Have a great day today. I love you. Do your best work. Do what your teachers say. Don't talk in class. Treat others how you want to be treated." The final sentence is a derivative of what we commonly call The Golden Rule. It comes from Luke 6:31 in the Bible where Jesus called followers to do unto others as you would have them do unto you.

These words are just as important in business as they are to my 10 and 14-year-old sons. How do you want your boss to treat you? Do you want him or her to be a cold, heartless, ruthless slave driver who pushes others beyond their limit to achieve an amorphous goal? Of course not. You want your boss to treat you how you want to be treated. You want her to care for your well-being, be humble, listen to you, have a coherent vision, and create opportunities that will allow you and your teammates to be as successful as possible.

Basically, you want your boss to be a servant leader and, given that's how you want to be treated, shouldn't you seek to be a servant leader to others?

How You Are at Home

I needed to hear Doug's advice on not eating boogers way back in the first grade. I had a problem. But I can't be the only one out there, right?

Joking aside, I am encouraged by the way Doug speaks to his young children before each day at school.

His example represents a difference in perspective that our country needs desperately. Truett Cathy, founder of Chick-fil-A, wrote a book titled "It's Better to Build Boys than Mend Men." What an amazing phrase for today's culture! Both in everyday society and in corporate America.

Doug's perspective on servant leadership starts in the home, and funny enough . . . I think that's where the heart of corporate America is won too. Whether you are a single individual crushing it in life, or a married spouse with five kids, I strongly believe that how you are at home impacts how you are at the office.

And when you start to falter at home you're likely to start faltering at the office. That may result in a kind of leadership style you never wanted to embody at the start of your career.

You Have a Choice (Doug Voss)

Leaders are important. *Someone* must hire and fire people. *Someone* must make any number of final decisions. *Someone* must formulate a vision. *Someone* must lead a team toward an ultimate vision.

Leaders are either chosen or called. Regardless of circumstance, the best leaders are those whose abilities match the moment at hand. For many, it takes only one or two of those big moments to earn the trust of individuals, leading a specific effort, organization, or even a Fortune 500 company. We are all equal under the law but our abilities are inequitably distributed. Given most tasks require a variety of skill sets, the most successful teams are those whose individual components have complementary skills, thereby creating a sum of greater parts than one's own. Someone must lead these teams, retain talent, develop talent, and steer a team toward an ultimate vision.

Employees are motivated to work for leaders who serve them, and vice versa for those who only serve themselves—at no greater time are we experiencing that reality than a post-2020 world. Employees all across corporate America are leaving employers who don't really care about them or their team as a whole. The key for any servant leader is perspective on the task at hand.

You've probably encountered a leader(s) who has little regard for their followers, and maximum regard for their own self-interest. This leadership style may work for a while. However, humans (and conceivably dogs, cats, giraffes, alligators, and most other living things) inherently dislike such leaders and don't want to stick with them . . . if they have a choice!

Choice is the key word here. Millions of Americans are finally waking up to the reality that they have a *choice*.

The cold, self-interested leadership style is only sustainable when employees are trapped in their positions. Employees in many industries are not trapped.

There is a labor shortage, and it is *extreme* in some industries. Employees can (and will) find different opportunities where they will be treated with respect and dignity. When given a choice between the uncaring leader and one who has an employee's best interests at heart, employees will choose the latter.

Employees prefer leaders who serve them on a regular basis, and the result is an employee who is fully committed towards achieving the goals set for them.

The Wisdom That Surrounds You

The perspective Doug brings to the table is one I hope leaders everywhere resonate with. Our country is at a crossroads regarding employee autonomy, and everyone's desire to dictate their own environment. Every business owner, executive, and leader needs to assess the role they've been playing and consider if that role is usually in the best interest of the *team* or merely himself or herself.

Every hard-working *employee* needs to assess the kind of person they want to work for, and what they strive to become through that experience. As I mentioned in the introduction to this book: you are the average of the 7 people you surround yourself with the most.

If one of those 7 is someone you work for and alongside on a day-to-day basis, I challenge you to consider if they're someone you want to work with for an extended period of time.

Care While You Can (Doug Voss)

Leading with a "caring" perspective deserves special emphasis. While humility is the foundation for servant leadership, caring is the bedrock upon which that foundation is built.

Some assume the role of servant leader for selfish reasons. That's fine. Servant leadership has been shown to improve morale, employee retention, and team performance. If you're the leader, each of those factors will make your work life better and help you progress your career. However, you must find it in your heart to care about your followers. Everything will fail if you're a servant leader without caring first.

I fail often—just ask any of my friends or family— but some things *do* come naturally to me. One of those is my propensity to say "yes" when asked to do something, which is a blessing and a curse.

I tend toward "yes" because I'm a people pleaser. Sometimes I say "yes" too frequently and make myself miserable because I'm at the whim of so many others. My mom was too. She would move heaven and earth to help others. She cared. My mom was a better person than I am, but I'm honored to say there was some trickle-down effect that I benefited from with her as my mother.

There are several techniques that may be helpful as you coach yourself to care or care more frequently. If you need a place to start, leaders must empathize with followers' problems. You probably have the same problems or know others who do. How would you want to be treated by your leader if you were in your followers' shoes?

Next, find peace in your life. You may do this through prayer, yoga, reading, running, or simply letting go of things you can't control. You can't care for others if your life is so chaotic that your brain only focuses on your own issues.

Finally, care for yourself. You're not perfect and no realistic person expects you to be. Look your faults in the eye, work on what you can, and embrace the rest. You must love yourself and be confident in who you are before you can care for others. Caring is where it all begins.

What Are You Working For?

When you choose to care about the success of others and put their goals, dreams, and ambitions ahead of your own, you will indirectly achieve all of yours. I've noticed that when I've put effort into getting to know my team, finding out what motivates them, and what their professional aspirations are I can help them accomplish their goals in a way that motivates them to work harder for themselves.

Your job has *to be* more than just a "job." We spend too much of our lives "on the clock" to wake up miserable each morning. If you do, it's an indicator that something has to change. Sure, that "change" could be looking for a different job/career path entirely, OR the change could come from within in terms of how you view and approach your current situation.

Let me ask you a question to round out Chapter 3: "What are you working for?"

Are you working so that you can make a bunch of money? Are you working so that you can fully put your skill set and passions to use on a day-to-day basis? Or are you working to provide for your family or put your kids through college someday? Are you mostly working for yourself or are you working for others?

There are no right or wrong answers to the questions above, but you might find that "What" we are working for quickly shifts into "Who" we're working for. But by "who" I'm not talking about your boss, I'm talking about the others in your life who you love, honor, respect, and long to support. In fact, your boss might be included in that last as well—if they're *not* in a list of those who you love, honor, respect, and support . . . *then* it might indeed be a time to make a change.

For an **"It's Not About Me"** mindset to occur, examine and take time to journal or think about the lives of those you're working for—naming those people and relationships will help you define an appropriate path forward and if a change in corporate America scenery is really necessary. Or if a deeper transition is called for: a change in perspective.

4

Sacrifice
WITH JIM HILDRETH

"Do not go where the path may lead, go instead where there is no path and leave a trail."
—Ralph Waldo Emerson

This quote means so much to me and it has had an incredible amount of influence on other writers, CEOs, business owners, employees, and any person that has influence over a group of people. Emerson's brief message on traversing such a path has an incredible amount of symbolism, irony, and foreshadowing—one chapter doesn't do it justice.

In 2019, I moved to Oklahoma to work for a separate branch within my company. One of the first colleagues I met was extremely nice and welcoming, and she mentioned her husband who was happy to help me move and transition into a new city. That colleague's husband is Jim Hildreth, and I was drawn to a friendship with him from the day we met. Although I wasn't thinking about "why" at first, I can now look back at those early interactions between Jim and I, and realize there were various qualities (within an "**It's Not About Me**" frame of mind) that drew me to him. Lo and behold, the more I learned about Jim and his background in the Army, the more I realized his learned experience through serving our country, impacted every day of his life. In other words, Jim was the kind of person I'd desire to be in that group of 7 individuals anyone spends most of their time with.

Spend enough time with a high-quality leader from our military, and you'll find the reason they're considered "high quality" (among yourself, peers, friends, or family) is because they live *sacrificially* in everything they do. From the moment they wake up in the morning it's not about them, but about serving those around them for the common good.

Jim's experience in the Army and lessons outlined below have immense potential in the corporate business realm. If you think managing people (or being managed!) is hard then take it from someone who did it with their own life as well as others on the line.

Jim did it for 30+ years. And if you want to enhance your skill set as a servant leader, consider some of his leadership experience below—boiled down to a few sentences after many faithful years of experience.

Thank you for your service, Jim. The world is literally a better place because of you.

Can't Lead Where You Won't Go (Jim Hildreth)

I have served as a leader in the Army from the lowest level as Team Leader all the way up to being an acting 1SG (First Sergeant) in charge of 350 soldiers. That "Team Leader" role occurred back in 1989 when I was promoted to the rank of Sergeant (E-5)—I was more-or-less a leader before my promotion, but pinning on my stripes made it official.

To acquire qualification as Non-Commissioned Officer (NCO) in the Army, I passed my promotion board—a bombardment of questions from the Senior NCOs in my Battalion—then completed a Primary Leadership Development Course (PLDC) to learn the types of leadership styles and processes of being a leader in the Army.

The day I pinned my stripes on, I was told by *my* 1SG something that has resonated with me every day of my life. He told me to always remember, as a leader, "You can't train what you don't know, and you can't lead where you won't go."

Those are words I have learned to fall back on during my time as a leader. Leadership in the Army is not an easy task but being a leader in general—from corporate America to little league sports—is not easy either. Everyone is watching you, because now you set the standard with everything word and action.

I always made a concerted effort to put my soldiers

first as a leader in the Army, which was taught to me in my time as a soldier and at PLDC. If you take care of your soldiers, they will in turn take care of you and the mission will get done.

Always Learning

To me, every good and strong leader is *always* learning. And there are three levels of leadership: below, same level, and above. All of us should not only occupy a little of each space at a time, but also assume the role of "learner" in the process—no matter which level you focus on at any given moment.

As it relates to corporate America, many businesses roll out "management training programs" with an intent to train and inform employees—these programs often come in the form of a book, series of videos, or in-person training lectures. But those programs can only teach so much. Let's turn back to the example of Jim in the Army.

When someone thinks about "basic training" in the Army, the first thing that comes to mind isn't necessarily a book, training video, or lecture series. Instead, "basic training" in the Army is learning through *doing the work* on a day-to-day basis, week after week. Is each day perfect? No. But striving for perfection each day is possible—soldiers call this "discipline" and that word has the ability to turn corporate America on its head. Discipline is a subset of servant leadership, and runs right in line with sacrifice alongside others. After all, in your current or future role, it's worth asking the question: who is going to build upon the groundwork I'm attempting to put in place?

Will They Lead When You're Gone? (Jim Hildreth)

The first taste of "servant leadership" (which wasn't widely used at the time) I experienced in the Army started with our leaders taking responsibility. At the time, we just referred to the principle as simply being a good leader and taking care of our soldiers.

Now, when I talk about taking care of our soldiers, that means everything from health, welfare, training, rewarding, and discipline. Not to mention general mentorship as they would strive toward success everyday in the Army.

My leadership style in the Army was to mentor soldiers in such a way that they could take my position at any time just in case something happened to me or if I was not around. I wanted them to know and understand how things were to be done for the sake of future missions.

Once you lead in a way that has a greater good in mind, even after you're gone, soldiers are more attentive and motivated since they can see how it's benefiting them to learn not only their job, but the jobs of the people around and above them.

Years after those first experiences, while serving as

manager for a defense contractor, the same processes applied—namely training and mentoring my people to take over my position—which motivated them to strive harder and do more without any type of coercion or threats.

Any leader in the Army is faced with many challenges when it comes to taking care of one's soldiers. Training stateside isn't *as* challenging, but when you deploy on a Training Mission, Peacekeeping Mission, or Combat Mission things get a little more complicated. And you need every member on the team moving as one under the direction of someone they know and respect—because he or she knows and respects the team.

Who Comes Next?

If you are reading this book, we need to wrestle with this reality together: we are all going to leave this Earth someday. For some, sooner than others. And I hope it's a long time before you have to confront that reality.

But once we acknowledge the aforementioned reality, we can act accordingly—how are we caring for and loving them so that this world is a better place after we're gone?

In the previous chapter, we talked about "how you are at home will largely affect how you are at the office" which is also true as it relates to legacy. Sacrifice starts in the home and caring for the people who care for you the most. After we leave our jobs, someone will replace us. But if you left your home tomorrow, who would replace you then? It's a sobering thought. Yet just a reminder that building future generations in the workplace is important, yes, but our local communities—family, friends, neighbors—is where true, lasting change will take place in the years to come. Will you play a part, or sit on the sidelines?

It's worth noting: "sitting on the sidelines" in life sometimes looks like attaining the business success you've always dreamed of.

Seize the Opportunity While You Can (Jim Hildreth)

A notable mission that highlights leadership challenges in real time came during a deployment to Iraq. I was serving on a Military Transition Team (MiTT) where we came alongside the Iraqi Army and tried to mentor them on ways to conduct missions, shoot weapons, and perform daily Army-type functions.

Our MiTT was made up of three Non-Commissioned Officers (NCO's) and nine officers . . . the cards were not stacked in our favor. I was the lead vehicle driver and my Truck Commander was a Colonel (0-6) and my gunner was a Captain (0-3). We made a very interesting group to say the least.

The rest of the team was arranged in the same way, except for our third vehicle—the other Sergeant First

Class (E-7) was the gunner, and he had an 0-3 driver and Truck Commander as well.

When building a team, many leaders go through a common series of events: form, storm, norm and perform. This sequence happened in Iraq once we arrived, and our "storm" phase hit right as we were relieving the outgoing MiTT.

It was a very painful and challenging process in itself, but add in the fact we were in a heavy combat zone multiplied the storm tenfold.

We finally worked through some communication issues to hit the norm and perform phases and had a successful deployment—for as emotionally bonding as those moments are, some guys you stay close with throughout the years and others you never hear from again.

Why highlight this snippet of military service when discussing leadership in corporate America? Well, that's easy to answer—leading with others in mind is nothing more than taking care of your people and things around them that would hinder or distract them from doing their jobs.

Being able to eliminate distractions helps create bonds between you and team members, and helps team members be more productive. Ultimately, eliminating distractions for your team makes work fun—a collective vision motivates team members to perform accordingly.

Warrior's Wanted

Ask yourself, are you living in a manner that leaves bread crumbs for whoever comes after to follow? Taking that a step further, how are we baking a loaf from scratch? Some employees are lucky enough to glean from bread crumbs left just for them. But how are we *really* setting up future generations for success? Are bread crumbs the best we can do? What would leaving a full loaf of bread behind look like in practice?

Alright, if I go any further with the bread analogy, this might turn into a cookbook. Which wouldn't be the worst thing in the world because **It's Not About Me** and if providing your family with a winning bread recipe helps feed your spouse and kids, then email me and I'd be glad to Google some recipes for you.

Prior to you sending that email, consider Jim's words on sacrifice today. To seize the opportunity while we can is what this life is about. But "seizing" obviously looks different for everyone. Instead of writing this book and telling you what to seize, I divert to a different call-to-action: go seize the relationships you've been blessed with. The important people in your life will carry you and your legacy much further than any month's-end sales quota will. Does this mean you shouldn't honor your role in corporate America and do the best you can at your job? Of course not. I want you to crush it in busi-ness, no doubt, but if you aren't prioritizing others in the process, then business success is merely chasing the wind.

Take a slogan out of the Army's book: "Warriors wanted."

I'm grateful to know one of those warriors in Jim Hildreth. And my hope is that we see a lot more like him pop up in businesses across the country.

5

Leading Questions
WITH BRENT WITTHUHN

"Optimism is the faith that leads to achievement. Nothing can be done without hope and confidence."

—Helen Keller

One of my mentors, Brent Witthuhn, altered the trajectory of my corporate career when he infused the power of "asking leading questions" into my day-to-day interactions. What started as a two-day training course turned into some of the most formative conversation I could have asked for as a young corporate professional. Asking leading questions is a way to not just achieve some kind of personal agenda, but ensure that employee-to-employee or employee-to-client interactions are performed in a mutually beneficial answer.

Brent gave me permission to dive into some of the principles he taught me in that two day span—in addition to writing a blurb in the following section about asking great questions in a leadership context. My hope, with the remainder of the chapter, is that you will catapult into a rich direction filled with meaningful relationships and a positive reputation in the business world.

Peel Back the Layers (Brent Witthuhn)

As a young leader, I had an education forged in permanent lessons that carved the path I am still on today. That education was making mistakes. I made so many mistakes and learned the hard way that leadership isn't about titles, money, management, compliance, ego, or the biggest office. A pillar of my leadership style is to make everyone around me the best version of themselves. One of the key components of this philosophy is to ask not only more questions but the right questions.

I developed a coaching style best compared to an onion. You see, just like humans, circumstances, sales, and business, onions are complex with multiple layers. Questions are the tools that uncover what is beneath each layer.

Before a leader can be a master of asking great questions, he or she must be a master of listening. To evolve from a transactional leader into a transformational leader I have found it is important to follow a few key steps:

1. **Focus**: Consider each conversation an opportu-

nity to make a deposit in the relationship. Don't listen to respond, listen to understand; then, peel back another layer.

2. **Ask More Questions**: Don't ask what time it is, ask how the clock is made.

3. **Repeat**: Repeat the issue at hand to confirm all parties are on the same page.

4. **Resolve**: Agree on the next steps to find a satisfactory conclusion to the issue at-hand. Who owns the next step? What is the follow up action item? How do we hold each other accountable?

The ability to ask questions that challenge your team while holding them accountable takes practice. We are practicing something with every conversation. Ask yourself: what have you been practicing?

Simple Strategy, Gargantuan Impact

There are a couple acronyms that you hear almost everyday in corporate America, and Brent's shared wisdom has a direct impact on both of them. The two acronyms are "CEO" (Chief Executive Officer) and "ROI" (Return on Investment).

Alright . . . so you might not hear these acronyms *every* day but they're definitely two of the more well-known terms tossed around in the corporate world. One is a title and the other is an expectation. One focuses on leadership and the other focuses on growth. The two go hand-in-hand, and both are CRUCIAL to the success or failure of any business. In other words, if there were a corporate "totem pole" with the most important terms and "things to know" I'm sure the CEO and ROI would be right at the top.

So, based on Brent's advice shared prior, I think it's appropriate to jump to the *base* of that totem pole: serving the customer.

To "serve the customer" gets at a core theme of this book: servant leadership. And yes, "serve" is obviously at the crux of both terms. Whereas CEO and ROI are two things you'll hear often in and around the office, "serving","service", or "servanthood" are *not* the norm. However, the few corporate offices in America that *do* implement a servant leadership mindset stick out like one of those throbbing thumbs Bugs Bunny took an iron to.

Those companies' *CEOs* often come all the way down from the top of the totem pole to serve their other leaders, employees, and customers. But again, those companies are rare. And it's also not worth assessing each move your CEO makes or all the things he or she could or couldn't do. Remember: **It's Not About Me,** and any attitude that stews about how your leaders do or don't lead well isn't helping anything. INSTEAD, I'd like to give you a different perspective and acronym to abide by.

L.I.S.T.E.N. and Learn

Forget the CEO. Forget the ROI. Because if you implement the following acronym on a regular basis, I'm willing to bet one of two things happens. Or maybe both!

1. When you L.I.S.T.E.N., your CEO will notice. He or she may not notice today, tomorrow, in a few months or in a few years. But there WILL be a ripple effect throughout the organization because you understand **It's Not About Me.**

2. When you L.I.S.T.E.N., your ROI will take care of itself. Instead of trying to crush your numbers and analytics on a regular basis, crush the following interpersonal qualities, in the form of a helpful acronym, and watch the numbers add up over time.

The L.I.S.T.E.N. acronym is something I came up with after heeding Brent's original stance on asking leading questions. Since developing the acronym, it's a way I can train and encourage others on a regular basis. A simple six-step formula that, who knows, may even lead to six-figure results.

Look 'Em in the Eye

Eye contact is so important. There's no other way around it. When you look someone in the eye, you honor and respect their dignity as a human. To give someone your full eye contact is to give them your full attention, and our current generation is experiencing a "test" like never before when it comes to who and what we give our attention to.

It is so easy, when dealing with a colleague or customer, to look right past them. And I don't always mean in a physical sense. With the people in front of us, we can mentally look past them onto the next thing. And oftentimes we feel like we're getting away with it! But more often than not, people in the corporate world know if you're truly engaged or kind of glazed over. Then, of course, we have something in all our pockets that are vying for our attention 24/7.

I'm not asking you to perfect this "L" in the weeks ahead, but I am asking that you start paying attention to *your attention*. Do you look others in the eye when they're across from you? Is your head constantly thinking about the next thing? Or do you silence all that is around you and inside you to give them your utmost attention. If **It's Not About Me**, then use each interaction you have to make it about them.

It's not the perfection of this attribute that makes LISTEN a success, but the pursuit of it will certainly set you up to perform the other five actions in a satisfactory manner.

Inquire About their Life

And we're back to asking leading questions. Boom!

But there's a caveat. Leading questions as it relates to work comes in a distant second to what matters most:

real life. Remember earlier when we discussed "how you are at home is how you are at work"? Well, if that is the case . . . then it's worth getting to know others' personal lives before jumping to work-related questions.

There are a few things to consider when inquiring about someone's life in the corporate world.

1. When first getting to know someone, it's important to not get too deep too quickly. Instead of inquiring about their health history or if they're working through any serious conflict with their siblings, keep it light. Sure, ask about their spouse, kids, or who they hang out with on a regular basis. Sometimes just a "tell me about your story" will give you quite a bit of background information as you're getting to know someone.

2. Take notes(mental or physical). They will likely include things like their spouse's or kids' names. They might drop a couple interesting tidbits about their story, and if you remember those things (and bring them up at a later date) that will go a LONG way with people. Mental notes are one thing, but consider writing them down in your phone contacts' "Notes" section.

3. Be open and vulnerable with them as well. Ideally, keep conversations at 70% *them* talking and 30% *you* talking. But when you do share about your life, be specific— it'll help them get to know you better and form a stronger connection.

When done well, those three sticking points will go so much further than standard small talk about sports and the weather. A personal connection first will lead to better business relationships thereafter.

Stick with Leading Questions

The more you practice L.I.S.T.E.N. in real life the more the whole thing will flow from start to finish. As it relates to the "I" and "S" of the acronym, asking leading questions about one's personal life will likely create better leading questions on the business side of things.

Instead of explaining this concept to you further, let's examine an example of a potential corporate interaction, and how positive interactions like it can make way for better business relationships.

Leader: "Hi Sarah! How was your weekend?"

Colleague: "Hey, thanks for asking. Unfortunately, my dad's test results came back and confirmed he does have cancer—like our family feared."

Leader: "Gosh. That's terrible to hear, Sarah. I'm sorry. Although I don't know him personally, I know many in our city who do and they always have great things to say about his role in their lives. Is there any way I can help you in the weeks ahead?"

Colleague: "That's nice of you to say. And thank you for the offer. But you know we're in a busy season, and I need to finalize these reports before sharing them with the team later this week."

Leader: "That makes sense. But how about this. Take today off. Go get some time by yourself or maybe call

your Dad to catch up. Go on a walk or whatever you
need to do to process next steps. We'll start finalizing the
reports so we can all hit the ground running tomorrow.
Don't sweat it."

Time to Listen

Life should dictate our work. Not the other way around.
In the aforementioned example, servant leadership is on
display when real life takes over. The fictional scenario is
a possible interaction during any given week in the
corporate world. So how will you react?

Leaders take time to listen. And in the example,
Sarah's response would likely cover two areas: 1) real life
and 2) real work. It's imperative you listen to others in
regard to both spaces.

She might come back with how much your suggestion means to her, and it's your job to listen and affirm
her. She might come back with instructions on where
those final reports are at, and then your team can fill in
the gaps accordingly.

It's all a matter of patiently listening—which is, right-
fully so, at the core of this L.I.S.T.E.N. acronym.

Establish a Plan

Sarah's example is a rather personal one. So let's look at
another possible conversation that leads to a vital step in
the process: establishing a plan.

Leader: "Hey Matthew. Good to see you this morning. How was the concert last night?"

Colleague: "Oh man, it was amazing. I've been a fan of theirs since high school and it was my first time seeing them live. My wife and I had a great time."

Leader: "Caroline is into the band as well?"

Colleague: "Man, she might be a bigger fan than I am. It was a really fun experience for both of us. But hey real quick I had a question. Before I send these invoices out at the end of the week to Nation Corp, do you want me to send them an email beforehand? Or just wait until Friday and send them all at once?"

Leader: "That's a good question. And I'm actually talking on the phone with Jim today from Nation Corp so I'll let him know you're preparing the invoices to send over. However, go ahead and send the email anyway. Keep it short. Just let them know the invoices will be in their inbox this week."

Colleague: "Got it."

Leader: "Yep. I'll let Jim know. You send the email to his team. Send them on Friday and then let me know once you do. I'll ping Jim on Friday afternoon and let him know you sent them. Thanks, Matthew."

Establishing a plan sometimes sounds redundant, but it effectively charts a path forward for you and your colleagues.

Although the CEO is tasked with establishing a plan on a macro level, executions of each plan on a micro level will ultimately contribute to overall success.

Next Day Follow Up

This last step in the L.I.S.T.E.N. process isn't imperative with every daily action you take, but boy it can take you far in the long run. Now that we've looked at two real world examples, let's look at two ways you could pursue "next day follow up."

Example 1

Sarah takes the day off. You charge your team with "filling the gaps" while she gathers herself and everyone agrees that's the right call. In fact, your leadership *energizes* the team to knock the final reports out of the park —finishing them in their entirety so that she hardly needs to do anything the next day she comes back to the office.

Your team has enough time to put a care package together for Sarah when she comes back the next day. One of Sarah's friends knows she likes anything from Target.
- Gift basket.
- Candle.
- Handwritten note.
- Her favorite candy.
- $50 gift card to take her Dad out to dinner sometime in the near future.

This kind of "next day follow-up" will reinforce to Sarah, and your team that life is more important than work. When those priorities are in order, work will take care of itself.

Example 2

The day after your interaction with Matthew you ask him about the invoices, and he tells you that Nation Corp said Friday is great. Jim told you thank Matthew on his behalf for his good work and prompt follow-up. Jim also tells you consistent communication like that Matthew is practicing makes you and your team a great business partner.

When a strong working relationship is in place, the bottom line numbers on an invoice hardly matter to the person paying it.

To live out **It's Not About Me on** a regular basis requires you LISTEN and ask leading questions. Every day. That's it.

You'll be surprised what the bottom of the totem pole can do, and how your actions will affect the rest of the whole damn thing. It's not a quick fix, but it's worth it in the end. Start putting L.I.S.T.E.N. into practice, and email me if you start seeing results. Sarah and Matthew's stories are interesting to me, but I wrote them into existence. I'd much rather hear how L.I.S.T.E.N. impacts you in real life.

6

Mistakes
WITH THREE GIANTS OF LEADERSHIP

"Your present circumstances don't determine where you can go; they merely determine where you can start."
　　—Nido Qubein

Every leader to some degree has made, or almost made a vital mistake that almost caused them to have to start over. In corporate America, there are too many leaders who have made too many mistakes to count. However, did you know that most Major League Baseball players who fail 70% of the time will likely end up in the MLB Hall of Fame? That's right. Most batters who end their career with a batting average of .300 or above will likely have a chance of a Hall of Fame induction.

Granted . . . leaders in business never *aim* to fail 70% of the time. It's just inevitable, on a daily basis, that we fail. We don't *always* hit our sales goals. We don't *always* make the right hire the first time.

The real leaders are those who can pursue success each day, experience *failure* each day, and keep moving toward the ultimate goal in the process.

The following sections are prime examples of historical leaders who did just that: set an ultimate goal, pursued success each day toward that goal, and ultimately experienced failure along the way. It's an inevitable journey, but if the goal is truly a mountain worth climbing, then failure will seem like an ant hill. How will you perceive those ant hills? As serious hindrances on your path, or expected bumps in the road? If you choose the latter, your day-to-day life in corporate America or any other job will be worth it. It's when you set goals the *size* of ant hills that life becomes about our own success and things we can attain here in life. With that said, what is a kind of goal that we *can't* attain in this life? In short, it's a goal that may only be realized until after we're gone from this place.

Each section that follows contains a lengthy passage from one of three individuals in history. There are many books and articles written about all three, so this is not my attempt to write their biography or highlight all of their life achievements. Instead, I picked three passages that spoke to an **It's Not About Me** mentality in the hopes of encouraging you to embody something similar. Often, we get Tweet-sized tidbits from those we look up to, but often miss the full context of why they said it. So to kick things off, let's look at an individual who chased a mountain size goal (and set of goals) that impacted generations beyond his time, and ultimately had an impact on, yes, even corporate America.

Abraham Lincoln (In His Own Words)

One-eighth of the whole population were colored slaves, not distributed generally over the Union, but localized in the southern part of it. These slaves constituted a peculiar and powerful interest. All knew that this interest was somehow the cause of the war. To strengthen, perpetuate, and extend this interest was the object for which the insurgents would rend the Union even by war, while the Government claimed no right to do more than to restrict the territorial enlargement of it.

Neither party expected for the war the magnitude or the duration which it has already attained. Neither anticipated that the cause of the conflict might cease with or even before the conflict itself should cease. Each looked for an easier triumph, and a result less fundamental and astounding. Both read the same Bible and pray to the same God, and each invokes His aid against the other. It may seem strange that any men should dare to ask a just God's assistance in wringing their bread from the sweat of other men's faces, but let us judge not, that we be not judged. The prayers of both could not be answered. That of neither has been answered fully. The Almighty has His own purposes. "Woe unto the world because of offenses; for it must needs be that offenses come, but woe to that man by whom the offense cometh."

If we shall suppose that American slavery is one of those offenses which, in the providence of God, must needs come, but which, having continued through His appointed time, He now wills to remove, and that He gives to both North and South this terrible war as the woe due to those by whom the offense came, shall we discern therein any departure from those divine attributes which the believers in a living God always ascribe to Him? Fondly do we hope, fervently do we pray, that this mighty scourge of war may speedily pass away. Yet, if God wills that it continue until all the wealth piled by the bondsman's two hundred and fifty years of unrequited toil shall be sunk, and until every drop of blood drawn with the lash shall be paid by another drawn with the sword, as was said three thousand years ago, so still it must be said "the judgments of the Lord are true and righteous altogether."

With malice toward none, with charity for all, with firmness in the right as God gives us to see the right, let us strive on to finish the work we are in, to bind up the nation's wounds, to care for him who shall have borne the battle and for his widow and his orphan, to do all which may achieve and cherish a just and lasting peace among ourselves and with all nations.

—*Lincoln's Second Inaugural Address*

Malice Toward None

There is one section in this book that is obviously not written during this millennium, and you just read it. Well, I hope you read all of it, because it's sheer gold. They just did it differently back then, and Abe was a cut above the rest.

Those 467 words were spoken by Abraham Lincoln on March 4th, 1865 at his second inaugural address. They weren't the only words he spoke, as I merely highlighted the second half of his speech. To many historians, these remarks rank right up with the Gettysburg Address. But many Americans today don't realize or consider the magnitude of this second inaugural address. You want to know something crazy about that speech?

Abraham Lincoln was assassinated 42 days later. Just five weeks after trying to make sense of a Civil War at the beginning of his second term in office. And he didn't mince his words!

At the start of this chapter, I mentioned mountain-sized goals. This speech addresses some of Lincoln's: namely, ending the Civil War and unifying a nation. Ending the war meant eliminating slavery which was obviously the mountain before him. Lincoln inherited over two-hundred years of slavery that permeated our nation, and his presidency saw a war break out over the horrendous issue.

"Both read the same Bible and pray to the same God, and each invokes His aid against the other."

Those words speak to the reality that we're all human, and nobody deserves to use one's power at another's expense—especially when a human's dignity and livelihood are at stake. And for as much as Lincoln's presidency is seen as a "success" when lined up alongside other presidents, he without a doubt faced many failures on his path toward achieving his goals. Much of Lincoln's failures were at the hands of human opposition, and those who told him he was pursuing a lost cause. And in the throes of war, he easily could've thrown in the towel. But he didn't—he kept going, committed to doing God's work set before him. The latter of which leads him to write a few words worth repeating:

"With malice toward none, with charity for all, with firmness in the right as God gives us to see the right, let us strive on to finish the work we are in, to bind up the nation's wounds, to care for him who shall have borne the battle and for his widow and his orphan, to do all which may achieve and cherish a just and lasting peace among ourselves and with all nations."

Those first eight words—"With malice toward none, with charity for all"—is another way of saying **It's Not About Me.** And the words that follow is his proclamation to KEEP GOING and finish the work you've been given. In corporate America, we get so caught up in daily numbers that we forget the bigger picture we're all a part of. It's not that our day-to-day is bad, but there is such an opportunity for *good* to pursue in and around our communities. In other words, there should be a deeper "Why" for all of us when we wake up each morning.

For Lincoln, it was about unifying a country—about securing *freedom* for every human being. For others, like the next two individuals in this chapter, it was about using that freedom and seizing the opportunities before us.

Malala Yousafzai (In Her Own Words)

When our bus was called, we ran down the school steps. The bus was actually a white Toyota truck with three parallel benches. It was cramped with 20 girls and three teachers. I was sitting on the left between Moniba and a girl named Shazia Ramzan, all of us holding our exam folders to our chests.

Inside the bus it was hot and sticky. In the back, where we sat, there were no windows, just plastic sheeting, which was too yellowed to see through. All we could see out the back was a little stamp of open sky and glimpses of the sun, a yellow orb floating in the dust that streamed over everything.

Then we suddenly stopped. A young bearded man had stepped into the road. "Is this the Khushal School bus?" he asked our driver. Usman Bhai Jan thought this was a stupid question, as the name was painted on the side. "Yes," he said.

"I need information about some children," said the man. "You should go to the office," said Usman Bhai Jan. As he was speaking, another young man approached the back of the van.

"Look, it's one of those journalists coming to ask for an interview," said Moniba. Since I'd started speaking at events with my father, journalists often came, though not like this, in the road.

The man was wearing a peaked cap and had a handkerchief over his nose and mouth. Then he swung himself onto the tailboard and leaned in over us. "Who is Malala?" he demanded.

No one said anything, but several of the girls looked at me. I was the only girl with my face uncovered.

That's when he lifted up a black pistol. Some of the girls screamed. Moniba tells me I squeezed her hand.

My friends say he fired three shots. The first went through my left eye socket and out under my left shoulder. I slumped forward onto Moniba, blood coming from my left ear, so the other two bullets hit the girls next to me. One bullet went into Shazia's left hand. The third went through her left shoulder and into the upper right arm of Kainat Riaz.

My friends later told me the gunman's hand was shaking as he fired.

—*I Am Malala* [1] *by Malala Yousafzai*

With My Face Uncovered

Wow. Where do you even begin in conveying the impact this young woman made on history? On the way she paved a path forward for millions of people?

Isn't it kind of crazy that two of the most memorable acts in the course of history took place on a bus: Rosa Parks and Malala Yousafzai. The former of which I could have written on as well, but I chose Malala for a couple reasons. On the one hand, Abraham Lincoln and Rosa Parks were obviously fighting a similar fight for a similar purpose: equal rights. Where Malala differs (although she's advocated for equal rights as well) is her age. Although she didn't realize it at the moment, during that fateful October 2012 bus ride alongside friends, Malala was going to change the world. (And what a way for the events to transpire: with her face uncovered, that was like a cultural stand to the men who attacked her that day). You see, where the men who shot her tried to "change the world" through fear, Malala was already changing the world through love.

In the months and years leading up to that moment, Malala (with the encouragement of her father and supporters around her) was advocating for educational rights for young girls like her—many of whom were facing persecution by the Taliban and other extremists.

Malala's fight was long and tedious until that day on the bus. The kicker is that men tried to end her life, but only increased her impact 1,000-fold. Through an incredibly miraculous turn of events, Malala lived through persecution and would go on to win the Nobel Peace Prize. Although Malala didn't experience "failure" at the hands of persecutors, it was instead the small failures she ENDURED until that point that makes her a hero today.

Yet another example similar to Lincoln's: leaders fighting through failure to achieve an end goal in mind.

The reality is that many of Lincoln's and Malala's failures we'll never know about. In fact, those "failures" rarely get written in history books. Make no mistake, these two individuals were human and made mistakes—they "failed" in a worldly sense on multiple occasions, but only continued because they believed their life mission was too important to give up along the way. In one circumstance, it was abolition of slavery, and in the other was rights to education. For both, they were rooted in an **It's Not About Me** mentality that carried them through failure.

For Lincoln, assassination was carried out in full. For Malala, assassination didn't prove as fatal. And in the end, both will be remembered throughout the course of history because of the way they laid their lives down so that others could not just live . . . but flourish.

So what does flourishing look like in real time? This next example is coming back a little closer to corporate America. Whereas Lincoln and Malala prove that pursuing a BIG goal is of utter importance, this next example proves that a rising tide certainly does lift all ships.

Mark Cuban (In His Own Words)

I read every book and magazine I could. Heck, three bucks for a magazine, twenty bucks for a book. One good idea would lead to a customer or a solution, and those magazines and books paid for themselves many times over. Some of the ideas I read were good, some not. In doing all the reading I learned a valuable lesson.

Everything I read was public. Anyone could buy the same books and magazines. The same information was available to anyone who wanted it. Turns out most people didn't want it.

I remember going into customer meetings or talks or go to people in the industry and tossing out tidbits about software or hardware. Features that worked, bugs in the software. All things I had read. I expected the ongoing response of: "Oh yeah, I read that too in such-and-such." That's not what happened. They hadn't read it then, and they still haven't starting reading it.

Most people won't put in the time to get a knowledge advantage. Sure, there were folks that worked hard at picking up every bit of information that they could, but we were few and far between. To this day, I feel like if I put in enough time consuming all the information available, particularly with the internet making it so readily accessible, I can get an advantage in any technology business. Of course, my wife hates that I read more than three hours almost every day, but it gives me a level of comfort and confidence in my businesses.

—How to Win at the Sport of Business: If I Can Do It, You Can Do It

Self-Educate. Win the Game.

Keeping this last excerpt short-and-sweet from Mark Cuban's *How to Win at the Sport of Business*. With a statement like this, Cuban empowers the reader with an admonition: learn everything you can to be as dangerous as you can. You know what made Abraham Lincoln and Malala Yousafzai so dangerous? They were self-taught. Lincoln read books non-stop during his upbringing, and so did Malala—one did because he didn't have technology as a distraction, and the other did because she didn't have another choice. Malala *fought* for her education on a more holistic level, but it does not mean she wasn't educated.

People look at Mark Cuban now and see a successful businessman. Mark Cuban looks at himself and sees YEARS of preparation, learning, and making time to be the best person he could be. Why? Because he understands **It's Not About Me.**

So what were his "failures" in the process? Well, this one's tricky because to educate oneself means sacrificing something very meaningful: time. To sit down and read a book means making time you could be doing other things like . . . golfing, or watching Netflix, or betting on sports, or the all-consuming scrolling social media/the internet. What will *you* value in the long run?

"Well isn't making time to educate myself 'making it about me'? What about an **It's Not About Me** mentality?'"

To answer the former: yes and no. Educating yourself is absolutely "about me." So that one might grow as a leader, and in Cuban's words, "get a knowledge advantage." However the end goal isn't "about me" at all—it's actually far better and more beneficial than that. You see, you can't help anyone else if your cup is empty. This Cuban excerpt is all about filling up your cup, on a regular basis, so that you can help others in the throes of corporate America. It is *not*, however, a quick fix solution. And you *should* expect to sacrifice your time (and sometimes general fun/enjoyment!) if you want to gain said "knowledge advantage."

Consider Will Hunting from the all-time classic, *Good Will Hunting*. Will is a character who did the work to attain self-knowledge, but struggled with next steps. He worked at night as a janitor (at a university) just so he could be close to academia and soak in second-hand knowledge as a result. But past that, he was kind of like a filled cup that just sat on the counter—nobody else was benefitting from all his knowledge because he was too afraid of change and where this "gift" might take him. Luckily, he had some best friends and a special mentor (all part of the 7 closest to him!) who encouraged him otherwise. In the end, Will's story is one of a rising tide that would lift all ships. When *you* get better, *others* get better. When you self-educate, you will win the game. It's all a matter of whether you're willing to put in the work, or resort to what's easy—the decadent society around you.

What if Lincoln hadn't educated himself? What about Malala? Had they not done the work to learn and grow as individuals, their "knowledge advantage" would never have taken root, and impact certainly would not have followed.

We're almost six chapters through this short book, but I understand this might be where I lose some people, because sitting down to actually do this work is HARD. It is not easy to gain this advantage over others. But in the end, it's *others* who will benefit from what you bring to the table. All you have to do is be willing to sit down with the text—the only thing left to decide is "Where do I even begin?" With so many great business and leadership-based books out there, it certainly is difficult to pick a starting point.

Lucky for you, I have a book suggestion that just might turn your business world upside down.

7

Wisdom

WITH KING SOLOMON

"Above all else, guard your heart, for everything you do flows from it."

—Proverbs 4:23

The book of Proverbs might get written off in a lot of corporate America circles because . . . well, it's in the bible. The book itself is a divisive thing. Even Jesus talked about coming to the world not to unify but divide.

But before Jesus made his grand entrance into this world, there was the book of Proverbs. And lest you think Proverbs, as a book, is more about *division* . . . think again.

Proverbs is all about the pursuit of wisdom. Think corporate America could do good by that? Absolutely. We all could. Wisdom isn't something you just attain one day—never having to seek it again. Wisdom is an everyday pursuit, and each verse in Proverbs helps people (at different parts of their journey) pursue wisdom accordingly. What do I love about each of them?

Proverbs are rooted in an **It's Not About Me** mentality. So much so that I had the most difficult time picking out a few to highlight in the ensuing sections. But I decided to first break it down into a few key categories: 1) Your Tongue, 2) Your Community, and 3) Your Integrity. Then, I observed each bit of wisdom and its direct correlation to the corporate America space. Was corporate America the original intended audience? Not quite . . . but that's one reason Proverbs are so impressive, is because the principles stated below are timeless.

In my humble opinion, the working world would do well to take *even just one* of the Proverbs below and apply it to one's leadership style. Better yet, consider how the following nine Proverbs might transform your workplace forever.

Note: The following Proverbs are all stated in the New International Version (NIV) of the bible.

Your Tongue

Those who guard their lips preserve their lives,
    but those who speak rashly will come to ruin.
    —Proverbs 13:3 (NIV)

The soothing tongue is a tree of life,

but a perverse tongue crushes the spirit.
—Proverbs 15:4

To answer before listening—
that is folly and shame.
—Proverbs 18:3

Two Ears. One Mouth.

Have you ever thought about that? That we have two ears for listening but only one mouth to speak. Maybe there's a reason behind that—to do a lot more listening than speaking. More on Proverbs 18:3 in a minute, but man oh man. Where to even begin with the aforementioned Proverbs?

I guess we start with the first one in the list:

Those who guard their lips preserve their lives,
but those who speak rashly will come to ruin.

Preserving one's lips is way easier said than done. We live in a day-in-age where pretty much "anything goes" in terms of water cooler talk or elsewhere in a work environment. But whether your speech is inappropriate while across from a colleague, or worse, behind his or her back . . . it is imperative to know that things will *not* bode well for you on the other side of unpreserved lips.

Each element of sarcasm, gossip, slander and more will effect your environment in a far more negative way than for some kind of "motivational" purposes. Guard your lips, because they're a surefire way to foster your culture in a positive light.

Your Integrity

> Whoever walks in integrity walks securely,
>   but whoever takes crooked paths will be found out.
> —Proverbs 10:9 (NIV)

> For lack of guidance a nation falls,
>   but victory is won through many advisers.
> —Proverbs 11:14

> It is a sin to despise one's neighbor,
>   but blessed is the one who is kind to the needy.
> —Proverbs 14:21

We Will Be Found Out

Maybe you've heard it this way: what is done in the dark will come to light. That line is true about all three of these Proverbs— each that has to deal heavily with one's integrity.

The words in Proverbs 10:9 should haunt leaders across corporate America. And lest you think "leaders" are confined to the C-Suite . . . nope. No matter your title in the organization, you have the opportunity to serve as a leader each day on the job. The real question is if you'll take advantage of that opportunity or not. Using the opportunity for good is the long, slow journey to making an impact. Taking advantage of them negatively is a strategy bent on instant gratification and an attitude that says **It *Is* About Me.**

But to choose the path that benefits *us* the most is often the "crooked path." And according to this Proverb, those who choose the crooked path WILL BE FOUND OUT. You may not be found out today, tomorrow, next month or even next year. Hell, you might not even be found out until you're old and wrinkly and have been retired for years. But the darkness will come to light eventually, and this Proverb reinforces that fact.

Instead, think about what it means to walk in integrity on a daily basis. What does that look like in life? In the business world, what *does* it mean to walk in integrity? All I know is that corporate America can be stressful enough—meeting deadlines, leading teams, landing the sale, and implementing new strategies on a weekly basis. To walk a crooked path makes all of those things even more stressful because you're working *extra* hard to conceal something in the dark. Do yourself a favor and expose the darkness for what it is . . . ASAP. What's a practical way to bring darkness to light? See the following Proverb.

For lack of guidance a nation falls,
  but victory is won through many advisers.

Wow. Many advisors . . . does that sound familiar? It

should—a variation of that statement was in the Introduction of this book: People are the **average of the 7 people they surround themselves with on a consistent basis.** (Aka "Many advisors"). If you neglect this principle—to invite wisdom in your life and give them permission to ask you the hard questions—you are headed toward a crooked path. The important thing is you identify who those people are and be transparent with them about your intentions: to invite sources of light into potential areas of darkness.

A practical way to do this is to assign leaders and mentors you know to help guide you in specific areas of life. For instance, who is someone you look up to in terms of their financial literacy and wisdom? Maybe you ask that person to meet with you once a quarter to discuss your finances and ways you can grow and give back to your community. Who is someone you know who is really good at leading people? Same thing. Ask if you can meet with them regularly to glean how you might lead others well, too.

When we pursue integrity as a means for personal and professional growth, the work we do all of the sudden becomes about *them*. "Them" in this instance is those you've been called to lead. After all, it's not just the leaders themselves who are affected by the proverbial crooked path . . . it's the people who are in that leader's sphere of influence. The storm affects us all, so calm the skies in the presence of a good community.

It is a sin to despise one's neighbor,

but blessed is the one who is kind to the needy.

"Kind to the needy" can change the world. But proceed with caution. If the goal of giving to the needy is so that others see your good deeds, think again. Giving to the needy should come from an overflow of good in your soul—not an overflow from your bank account. In other words, Proverbs 14:21 isn't just for philanthropists in and around corporate America. This verse is for all those who, again, seize today as an opportunity for good and making an impact right where they are.

Your Community

Those who work their land will have abundant food,
    but those who chase fantasies have no sense.
—Proverbs 12:11 (NIV)

It is a sin to despise one's neighbor,
    but blessed is the one who is kind to the needy.
—Proverbs 14:21

Kings take pleasure in honest lips;
    they value the one who speaks what is right.
—Proverbs 16:13

Be Kind. Be Focused.

To implement an **It's Not About Me** mentality is to, in the end, form and cultivate a special kind of community. These last three verses exemplify an honorable kind of community in full. Before a quick word on each, it's important to note how the first Proverb (12:11), from a business standpoint, can be channeled through internal operations—same goes for the third Proverb (16:13). But the *middle* Proverb (14:21) will shape the way your business operates on an external level.

Proverbs 12:11 contains a phrase that might stick out to many leaders in corporate America: "chase fantasies." What I love about this Proverb is that it cuts to the heart of a problem our country is currently facing: The American Dream 2.0.

What do I mean by "The American Dream 2.0"? Well, everybody is familiar with The American Dream—house, job, family, car, kids, dog, etc.—and, quite frankly, there is nothing inherently wrong with any of those things. But where such an idea was made popular in a post-World War II era, and lasted for decades . . . it's just not enough anymore. Today, The American Dream 2.0 looks *somewhat* like the original version, but it's also where "chase fantasies" comes into play and why everyone needs to stay alert and stay focused.

The American Dream 2.0 looks a little bit like a house but a lot like a yacht. The American Dream 2.0 looks a little bit like a job but a lot like a six-figure salary with plenty of benefits and bonus structures. The American Dream 2.0 looks a little bit like a car but a lot like an $80k electric vehicle. The American Dream 2.0 looks a little bit like a family but a lot like autonomy to still do and fulfill each of our personal pleasures.

But to actually *"work the land"* means waking up everyday to do the work, love your neighbor, and make the world a better place. What's the reward? Abundant food. Or in other words, "our daily bread." Is that enough for us? And if not, what's the alternative? Although The American Dream 2.0 and the fantasies that come with it *seem* appealing, in the end . . . they never satisfy quite like we think they will.

Which is a great segue into Proverbs 14:21: *"Blessed is the one who is kind to the needy."* Not to completely skip over the first part, which talks about despising one's neighbor as sin. Man! What a wild and antithetical statement compared to the aforementioned American Dream(s). What would it look like if our yachts looked more like more vacation time for the whole company? What would it look like if our salaries looked more like bonus opportunities for *other* employees? What would it look like if money toward a new car went to a local food shelter?

Again, this middle Proverb is more external, as loving one's neighbor means better communities across America. It's not a *quick* fix, but it's certainly a *better* fix than the ones we chase for ourselves.

And lastly, a Proverb that includes a very interesting

term: "King." In corporate America, we might see that word and automatically associate it with our boss. Or *the* boss. The CEO or person we report to. On the other hand, we might see *ourselves* as the "King" in this Proverb—we want others to be honest with us and tell us all those things that seem right to us: numbers are up, ROI is looking good, capitalizing on margins, hiring the right people, and so on. But whether you take this Proverb as the former or latter, consider a third option . . .

Our neighbor is the King, and out of a servant leader's heart we will speak what is right unto others. We will check dishonesty, malice, and gossip at the door.

Whether that door is at work, at a client's office, or definitely at home—may servant leadership carry us into everything we do. The book of Proverbs knows that wisdom is an **It's Not About Me** mentality, and many more verses speak to that reality. I just chose a few, but I'd love to hear about *your* favorite Proverbs and why they mean a lot to you. Maybe you take Proverbs and apply them at work, or maybe you keep them oriented on a personal pursuit for wisdom. Either way, don't overlook this book that's been working for thousands of years in favor of a self-help book that's been a bestseller for a few years.

As for this book you hold in your hands, my hope isn't a text that sticks around for a couple thousand years. But you know what? Maybe a couple thousands people will be impacted by your life as a result of working through these pages in a short book about servant leadership in corporate America.

Will you reach all those people in a few months time? Probably not. (But maybe! Maybe you're lucky enough to be in a position to do so). The real impact is made by, again, waking up every day and working the land you've been given. The result will surprise you.

The Result

Because that's what corporate America is all about, right? The result!

What's the end result for the company? What's the end result for the customer? What's the end result for *me*? Millions of Americans wake up each day with questions like these on their minds.

But the long-lasting results will carry you farther than any dollar bill or crypto currency ever could.

What about legacy? What about serving my neighbor? What about the people who might carry my casket some day?

Man. *That* escalated quickly. But for good reason. Because in the same way this book started with 7 people, it's going to end with 7 people—those who might indeed be at your funeral. What might they say about you as a person? How did you impact them? What were your results in *their* life?

This somewhat morbid reality is actually a pretty good way to live each day of your life, thinking about the future—the farthest our future might extend, which culminates in a day where friends and family gather to talk about the way you woke up each morning and went to work.

Not for you. Not for the company. But for others.

Because **It's Not About Me.**

Or should it be?

Afterword
DANGER IN THE DARKNESS

The 7 Principles/Chapters above, when implemented over an extended period of time, form a solid foundation for servant leadership in the workplace—and in the context of this book, for corporate America.

The final question in Chapter 7 is a bit of a mind bender, but let me tell you this . . . it's for a good reason. I just spent a whole book telling you how **It's Not About Me** only to pose the question, "Or should it be?" right at the end.

Well, there is a lot more to come on this front, but all of it, again, stems from my time and experience in corporate America. This book was filled with a lot of positivity —positive leadership traits and examples from leaders themselves. I did this on purpose, because there is inherently so much negativity in the workplace. You don't have to explain away how dark it can get inside corporate America for a number of reasons. Is it all bad? Of course not. I have met some of the best men and women during my time in the corporate world, and I obviously asked a few of them to join me in this authorship journey.

As for the pitfalls of this world . . . it really does make you think: how is this sustainable? Waking up, on the grind, day after day, sacrificing your time, and perhaps engaging in a line of work that just does not bring you fulfillment. AND, to continue on with that cycle (pouring yourself out to others) without filling yourself up with life and joy will eventually lead to what we call "burnout" or sometimes worse—a full on tailspin out of control. That, my friend, is what we call darkness. And when there is immense darkness, guess who it *should* be about. You. *That's* when "It *is* About Me" isn't just okay to say, but is okay to enact. *That's* when you need to step back from the grind and examine your life in extreme detail. And *That's* when you need to start looking at what you're prioritizing in this life.

Because when the darkness reaches its most pitch-black moment, and you don't think you can take another day, it's important to remember one of the greatest phrases ever uttered . . .

Let There Be Light.

Acknowledgments

I would like to thank…

My beautiful fiancé, Katlyn, who I look forward to spending the rest of days with. I'm so glad that God helped me find you. I can't imagine my life without you in it. I love you.

My little ones, Noah and Audrey. Thank you for being patient with me while I learn to lead you both. We are going to have so much fun together and I can't wait to watch you grow up. I love you both.

My brother, Michael, who at the end of any day has my back. I love how our friendship has evolved over the years. I'm proud of the man you've become.

My parents, Greg and Lina, who spent their lives giving and teaching me to become who I am today.

My Grandpa, Ralph, who is one of my idles and inspiration day in and day out.

My friend and mentor, Dan Augustine, who gave me the first big job in my life. He not only taught me how to do it, he coached me patiently when I struggled with it. He helped me with personal and professional struggles that I had.

My friend and editor, Will Severns, who talked with

me about the project at all hours of the night. He went to Miami with me to bring this project over the finish line. Without Will, I wouldn't have this book.

My friend and coach, Alex Demczak, who helped me get in touch with the right people and continues to guide me in my path to becoming a speaker.

My friend, Damon West, who's book and conversation started this entire project.

My friend and partner in crime, Frank Pruss. Frank and I hit it off instantly the first time I met him. He has answered the phone at all hours of the day. He and his family have always been there for me.

My friend, Austin Hoelzeman, who flew across the country to help me move home. He and his family have always welcomed me into their home.

My friend and mentor, Brent Witthuhn, who believed in me when a lot of people didn't. Thank you for your lessons and friendship over the years.

My friends John Pangle and Tanner Chapman for teaching me how to learn from mistakes. It's one thing to point out mistakes, but it is friends that truly care to teach you how to overcome that.

My teachers and college professors that made an impact in my life. I learned something from every single one of you.

Last and not least, God, for putting all people and events that have transpired so far in my life. Every single event has created the person you see today.

Notes

6. Mistakes

1. *Yousafzai, Malala, 1997- author. I Am Malala : the Girl Who Stood up for Education and Was Shot by the Taliban. New York, NY :Little, Brown, & Company, 2013.*

Made in the USA
Columbia, SC
07 December 2023

27221850R00054